Surviving and Enjoying Your Adolescent

The Coping Parent Series:

Surviving and Enjoying Your Adolescent———

I.J. Barrish, Ph.D.
Harriet H. Barrish, Ph.D.

Foreword by
Raymond DiGiuseppe, Ph.D.

Cover by: Ken Walker and Matt Moore
Text layout: Noelle M. Kaplan, finedesign

ISBN 0-933701-42-X

Printed in the United States of America

Library of Congress Cataloging-in-Publication Data

Barrish, I.J., 1945-
    Surviving and enjoying your adolescent / I.J. Barrish, Harriet
Barrish.
        p.   cm. — (The Coping parent series)
    Includes bibliographical references.
    ISBN 0-933701-42-X: $7.95
    1. Adolescence.   2. Adolescent psychology.   3. Parenting.
I. Barrish, Harriet H., 1945-   .   II. Title.   III. Series.
HQ796.B294   1989   89-38432
155.5—dc20   CIP

We are grateful to Bradley, Jonas, and Brandy,
who share with us their lives
and increasingly their adolescence.

Table of Contents

Foreword

Jay and Harriet Barrish have done it. They are surviving their children's adolescence successfully. And with years of clinical experience they have helped many other parents do it as well. Now they have organized the information they have used into a helpful book for parents. Up until now most books written by psychologists on parenting have focused on what parents can do to influence their children. While this type of book has helped many parents it has also lead to considerable anxiety. Today's parents know that they have to do the right thing by their children. And, if they don't, some therapist will have to undo the damage in the future.

What is unique about this book is the focus on parents' feelings about parenting and their children. We all have learned that we get our deep-seated emotional problems from our parents. Most therapists focus on how we feel about our parents. But I have always found that the strongest emotions experienced by myself, my friends and my clients are the emotions about our children. The greatest sadness, joy, fear, or remorse you will feel is probably going to be about your children. This seems obvious to any parent who sees their child suffer, or regrets not doing the right thing, or sees their child thrive. It just has not been obvious to the psychologist. Parents are rarely described as having emotions when it comes to performing the job of child rearing.

Psychological research has almost exclusively focused on how parents effect their children, and what the parent can do to improve the child's development. But what about the effect of having a child upon the adult? Nothing changes one's life like the arrival of an infant. And there are no operating instructions! What should one do? When do you give them freedom? How much homework should they do? So many questions and so few answers. And if your child should have troubles? Well, everyone knows it's the parents' fault. The psychoanalysts say it's because of a poor parent/child relationship. The family therapist says it's the child's attempt to maneuver around the parents' disturbed marriage. The behavior therapists say it's because the parents were ignorant of the right child-rearing skills. There is a lot of parent blaming which goes on among the mental health professionals. All of the confusion, the ignorance, the fear, and the love add up to some pretty intense emotions.

Surviving and Enjoying Your Adolescent helps parents deal with these strong emotions. It is written not only with the noble intent of helping parents raise a more adjusted adolescent but with the additional resolve of making the parent's life more enjoyable as well. The Barrishs have expanded the work of the renowned psychologist Albert Ellis. Ellis is the founder of rational-emotive therapy, a brief, highly efficient form of psychotherapy. The principles of rational-emotive therapy state that people can control the type of emotional reaction they have to situations by the way they think. Logical, rational, realistic and scientific thinking leads to appropriate functional, emotional reactions. Illogical, irrational, unrealistic, and unscientific thinking leads to disturbed, dysfunctional emotions. In order for parents to behave adequately as parents they must first be undisturbed emotionally.

Anger, fear, or guilt usually influence parents to behave in ways that are destructive to the adolescent's development. Parental emotional control will then allow better judgment in parenting. This will occur if the parents are accepting of the adolescent and accepting of themselves. Demanding that our adolescents be perfect, reasonable people who present no problems for us would be nice. But it would not be reality. Adolescents have this bad habit of growing up to be different from the way their parents want them to be. They develop their own desires, tastes, and styles. They are not always what we would like them to be. The rational attitude for parents is to accept your adolescent the way they are. By *accept* we do not mean that you must approve everything they do. By *accept* we mean that you acknowledge the way they are and work from that fact. Also, rational parents do not condemn their adolescent for being different but acknowledge their worth as a person even though they may have turned out different from earlier expectations. Parents also will benefit emotionally from accepting themselves with their faults and failings as a parent. Again, by *accept* we mean acknowledge your failings and work at improving them, not at downing yourself. Once parents can accept they cannot be (and probably are not) perfect parents they will be more emotionally in control and will make better judgments about parenting.

Raymond DiGiuseppe, Ph.D., ABPP, ABBP
Institute for Rational-Emotive Therapy
New York, New York

Preface

This book represents a natural blending of a sympathetic understanding of adolescent development with a **cognitive behavioral** approach to coping skills. This natural synthesis evolved as we fused our strong developmental background and understanding with our continuing growth in cognitive-behavioral psychology. We realized that the first step in helping parents cope with adolescence was to help them more fully understand about this developmental period. From Dr. Albert Ellis and Rational Emotive Therapy we got the elegant coping statements "They should act this way", "This should be happening", "They can act this way." Knowing what to expect developmentally from adolescence increases the chances that these coping statements can be made by parents.

Approaching adolescent development as Dr. David Elkind does, with understanding and in a sympathetic fashion, also sets the stage for improved coping by parents. We view coping skills for parents as critical to the development of relationship and **closeness** between parent and teenager. Parents who cope are much more likely to be in charge of their own emotional reactions to what their adolescents do. Learning not to be reactive as a parent while having a sympathetic understanding of adolescent development sets the stage for having a strong relationship with a young person. A close relationship during adolescence is protective of both parent and child. It protects parents because it allows them to have a real and influential involvement in the lives of their adolescent. A strong relationship, in our opinion, is the best insurance a parent can have against serious problems during adolescence. For a young person, a strong relationship ensures continuing adult support and feedback at a time when guidance is critical in making choices. Without emotional closeness and a strong relationship, adolescence is a time of increased conflict, turmoil, and division.

We view adolescence as a wonderfully unique era. With perspective and a sense of humor, parents can enjoy this unique developmental period. Adolescents continue to need a close loving relationship with their parents and it is our view that, because parents are the designated adults in this formula, it is up to them to do their best to learn and know how to make themselves the best they can be for themselves and their children.

Acknowledgements

This book could not have occurred without the sharing of the many teenagers and their families with whom we have had the privilege to work. Each in their own unique way added to our collective understanding and appreciation of adolescence.

We also acknowledge a debt of gratitude to *Twins Magazine* and especially Barbara Unell who allowed us to use parts of articles Dr. I.J. Barrish wrote for *Twins* adolescent column.

The work of Dr. David Elkind and his sympathetic understanding of young people has been influential in the development of our blend of developmental psychology with cognitive-behavioral psychology.

We continue to be indebted to Dr. Albert Ellis for his role in our professional development. We also continue to appreciate the support of the Institute for Rational-Emotive Therapy and especially Dr. Ray DiGiuseppe who has always been a friend as well as a colleague.

The Departments of Psychology and Human Development at the University of Kansas and especially Doctors Don Baer, Montrose Wolfe, and Frances Degan Horowitz helped us develop a richer appreciation for developmental psychology.

We also continue to be grateful to our friend and colleague Dr. Edward Christophersen, who, as always, encourages, advises, and supports us. Dr. Christophersen's colleagues, Drs. Mike Rapoff, Linda Ross, Martye Barnard, Vinnie Barone, Jan Myers, Judy Mathews, George Williams, Pat Friman have all offered terrific support of our work with adolescents.

We continue to be indebted to Dr. Jan Roosa, who early on in our professional development presented his professional model of a sympathetic understanding of adolescence.

As always we continue to appreciate the support, advice and caring of our colleague, Dr. Gerald Vandenberg.

We acknowledge a large debt of gratitude to Trudy Galblum who did research and the original manuscript of the chapter "What is Normal." We are also grateful to Ann Wilke who assisted in rewriting this transcript so it would be more readable for parents and to Barbara Cochrane for her editorial assistance. Our thanks extend to Jean Harmon who assisted in the preparation of the manuscript.

I.J.B.
H.H.B.

Chapter 1

Adolescence:
Coping With The Big Change

Change and adolescence.

Like salt and pepper, nachos and cheese, roses and thorns, change and adolescence go together. This is a fact of life.

Change can be exciting, often challenging, sometimes frightening both for the adolescent and for the adolescent's parents swept up in it. That is another fact about change — it cannot be ignored.

Change can, however, be met with less fear and more confidence. The tool that makes the whole experience less fearsome is information — specifically, information about adolescent development. Adolescents, after all, are still developing. Boy, are they!

Their developmental path is a rocky one from childhood to adulthood. The great thing is that, rocky as it may be, this is a path well trod. We've all gone through it; there are signposts, markers to expect.

If a parent can see that the phrase , "It's all part of growing up," really does apply, then perhaps a particularly annoying or upsetting adolescent act will seem less threatening. What the kid is doing is not personal — it is developmental.

It's time to give you examples. The list is good-sized.

Does your adolescent wish you were invisible sometimes? Is he or she more close-mouthed than you remember from the third-and fourth-grade years? Is your adolescent embarrassed by your home, clothes, car (fill in your own blank)? Does he or she question your values? Care less about academics? Care more about a good social life?

All this is just a sampling of typical adolescent behaviors. All developmental.

Okay. So you can accept that these behaviors, albeit unpleasant, are part of the passage. That does not mean — repeat, **does not mean** — you have to ignore or condone the poor choices, the disagreeable acts. No, no, no.

To accept means only to acknowledge that something is happening and that it is not unusual. It's like any other problem you meet in your life; you can better deal with it once you have accepted that it exists and that it is part of being human.

Next step? Do something about it. Form a plan of action. That is something you can do with your adolescent. Let your feelings be known. Your acceptance of unpleasant behavior can help shield you from severe emotional upset. Acceptance does not mean you agree with the unpleasant behavior or like it occurring. Acceptance shields parents from emotional upset because parents don't get as emotionally upset inside when they accept an unpleasant situation. Acceptance will free you in difficult situations to communicate more positively with your child.

If your teenager is exploring alcohol use, for example, accepting that this is likely to occur (93% of high school seniors have explored alcohol use sometime during their high school career) is not the same as liking it, agreeing with it, or feeling happy about it. Accepting does not mean parents won't fully share their feelings. However, acceptance implies that often parents don't have control over what their son or daughter does once they've left the house. It is better to accept what you don't control because the acceptance sets the table for having parental INFLUENCE.

There are some nice side effects to learning and practicing this brand of acceptance. For one thing, it sets an example. A parent who can accept and cope is more likely to have offspring who can accept and cope. Kids watch their parents' behavior. When parents accept, cope, and deal with situations, kids tend to incorporate what they see their parents doing into their own behavior.

If a young person watches a parent calmly problem solve their way through a situation instead of blaming others or procrastinating, he or she is more likely to catch on to problem solving, to figure out what the options are, and to determine what consequences are connected to each option than to blame, to get depressed, and to avoid. And — while you are practicing acceptance of your adolescent as an adolescent — practice some inward acceptance of you as you. It's the same ball game. You can accept yourself as worthwhile and valuable and still recognize your mistakes. With that acceptance of self, the mistakes and poor judgments and bad choices are fixable.

Special attention has to go to parents with several adolescents in the family. Multiple adolescents — multiple challenges. Odds are that one of those teenagers is probably giving you more trouble than the others at any given time. The temptation is to get angry with the problem-maker. Sentences like, "Why can't you be more like your brother?" escape the lips.

Avoid the anger. And the comparisons. Both tend to invite resistance — and damage brother-sister relationships at the same time. Each teen is traveling through adolescence at his or her own pace, passing through stages of development at different times, responding in different ways. Each is a distinct and special individual.

So much is going on — so much to remember. How do we cope?

Talking to yourself can help, whether you are the parent of one or many teens. Internal conversations that are rational are a proven coping device.

Instead of telling yourself that the latest incident, misjudgment or action is a catastrophe or an awful, terrible, horrible, devastating event, tone down a bit. Maybe, could it instead be unfortunate? Perhaps disappointing? Inconvenient? Regrettable? Tone down your assessment of the situation and you will probably be able to tone down your feelings. Your reaction will be less intense, more matter-of-fact. What we say to ourselves affects both our emotions and our acts.

Another help for parents is some examination of our own tolerances. Take time to consider the difference between what you don't like and what you can't stand. If you can't stand something, that means you really cannot tolerate it.

What things might your teenager do that you really and truly cannot tolerate? How are those things different from the things he or she does that you don't like?

When you say to yourself, "I can't stand that," then your level of frustration is probably low and your capacity for becoming angry or upset is probably high.

Part of the developmental process, part of growing up is making mistakes. Teenagers will make errors in judgment. They will violate your rules and guidelines. Recognize that and your reactions are less likely to explode into overreactions.

However, recognizing that fact of life will not keep you from disliking a misdeed or from implementing some consequences. Anger has nothing to do with applying consequences. In fact, the two must be kept separate. If they are not, the typical teenager will react to the anger. The reaction is apt to be so strong that the parent-sent message or consequences will be missed.

The biggest danger of all for a parent trying to cope with a teenager is confusion about your own self-worth. Your parental and personal worth are **not** determined by what your teen does at school or around town or at home. Be happy about his or her performance when it is good, and be helpful when it is not. Do not fall into the trap of believing that you are a better person because your teen did well or that you are a lesser person because he or she did not.

When you link your self-esteem with your child's performance, everyone suffers. You overreact, the child feels pressured, everyone rides a roller coaster. All gets blown out of proportion. Remember — adolescence is a time when it is normal for a human to be reactive, rebellious, confused, and prone to make errors.

Kids and parents are both fallible. You will make mistakes. So will they.

Know that you are fallible but unique and very worthwhile. Sometimes you may be better at this parenting business than at other times. But your worth is never diminished by your adolescent's mistakes or your own mistakes. Nor is your worth enlarged by your adolescent's successes. So, if your son or daughter gives up an activity like tennis, scouts, or violin or gets kicked out of class or off a team, his or her worth or yours remains unchanged.

Each of your adolescents is a unique and worthwhile person who will sometimes perform well and sometimes disappoint. Whatever the case — his or her inherent worth is not changed. And your worth is not measured in the balance of his or her performance — not ever!

Another key ingredient for better coping is to make sure you nurture and protect your relationship with your spouse. Taking time to strengthen this relationship will give each of you more strength and resiliency when dealing with difficult moments with your adolescent.

If you are a single parent it is especially vital for you to practice being good to yourself. This includes developing strong support systems, time off from a full-time parenting role and sufficient rest.

A final word about surviving and coping with the teen years as a parent. A sense of humor is required equipment. Some of these situations — as maddening as they are — are worth a chuckle, or at least a smile. Practice stepping back and seeing the humor in the situation, in your teen's behavior, in your own.

Learn to laugh — often silently.
Oscar Wilde said it well...
"Life is too important to be taken seriously."

Chapter 2

What Is Normal?

Knowing what to expect from a new experience is the first step toward handling the new experience. When parents are prepared for childbirth they are taught about labor and delivery. They go to the hospital, see the labor and delivery room, and are taught to fully understand what will happen when it's their turn. Knowing what is to come reduces fear and increases confidence. So it is for the parents of adolescents. Knowing something about typical adolescent feelings and behaviors gives parents the advance notice they need.

Adolescence is undeniably a turbulent time of development. Much adolescent behavior that seems bizarre and highly aggravating is developmental—not pathological or personal. Knowing what is to come helps us to set realistic expectations. In addition, our parental standards can be readjusted based on what kids can be developmentally expected to do at any given developmental point in time.

That is not to say that everything happens with everyone at the same time. Not at all. All development occurs on an individual continuum; not all adolescents will have the same experiences, respond in the same way, or feel the same intensities.

Dr. James Gardner has a good and applicable phrase: "normally disturbed adolescence." Those parents who recognize the earmarks of "normal disturbance" are much less likely to overreact to their

7

adolescents. Without overreaction, understanding is more apt to happen and, with that, the parent-adolescent relationship can remain intact.

Adolescence has changed considerably in the last century. It begins earlier and lasts longer. One hundred years ago the average age for the onset of puberty in girls was 16 years old; today it is 12 1/2 years old.

One of the reasons that adolescence begins earlier now is that young people have greater exposure to language, images, and understandings because of mass media. In addition, as a society we seem to encourage young people to grow up more quickly, and place a lot of pressure on them to learn things at a younger age, to be more athletic, and to be more competitive. Society generally gives the message to them that it is preferable to grow up more quickly.

Although puberty starts earlier, the change into adult roles comes later. The need for more post-high school education keeps adolescents away longer from the adult world of career and family. More widespread affluence makes it easier for parents to support their adolescent offspring longer. The time of dependence upon parents increases.

The physical, emotional, and intellectual changes of puberty when combined with social demands, cultural confusion, and vocational uncertainty results in high levels of stress for adolescents.

There are several dimensions of adolescent development and "normal disturbances" that characterize each dimension.

Intellectual Development

The physical changes of puberty are the most obvious. Equally remarkable, however, is the significant growth in mental capacity which occurs at this same time.

Swiss psychologist Jean Piaget, a man known for his theories on the development of children's cognitive abilities, identified adolescence as a period which heralds "formal operational thought." This thinking ability is the basis for all forms of higher level reasoning: conceptualization, logic, abstraction, propositional thinking (the ability to speculate on how things might be as opposed to how they are).

No longer fixed in the concrete, the literal, and the present, the adolescent begins to consider ideals. He or she begins to ponder.

That pondering forms the basis for criticism.

Adolescent intellectual development includes some common manifestations.

Idealism. The person who can envision what might be can also see his own world as something less than perfect.

That perceived gap between the real and the ideal often leads to harsh and seemingly unfair criticism, particularly in early adolescence. When focused on self, the adolescent finds fault with his or her own weight, height, hair, skin, facial features, and body size. When focused on family, he or she may find parents a source of extreme embarrassment — for almost any reason.

In later adolescence, more sophisticated, critical, and idealistic expression may be directed toward religion and politics. Now comes the recognition of a distinction between religion as an institution and religion as a personal commitment to a set of beliefs. Now comes also the realization that religious institutions have flaws.

This thinking leads many adolescents to question every aspect of their parents' religious convictions and practices. It may lead them to rejection of those convictions and practices. Many older adolescents also become very sensitive about hypocrisy in others. (Few, however, recognize the inconsistencies between their own actions and professed beliefs.)

The process of questioning, seeing hypocrisy, and rejecting family values is part of the process of the development of identity during adolescence. Trying on different identities and values leads young people to flirt with different hairstyles, clothes, choices, and peer groups. The process of identity development is part of adolescence. It is to be expected in some form. I can remember during my own adolescence questioning the authority and values of parents and significant adults. I also vividly remember practicing to walk like Paul Newman, wearing my hair long like the Beatles, and buying my clothes at thrift shops as part of my own journey through identity.

This time includes beliefs about how the world should be. Kids are idealistically comparing the reality they encounter to their perception of the perfect world. Sometimes this process can lead to real disillusionment because young people don't realize that their perspective will change with time. At times, the discrepancy between the real world they see and the perfect world they want can lead them to feelings of depression and hopelessness. I can remember meeting a young person who became very aware of environmental issues; her awareness led her to believe that adults had, by their negligence, destroyed the oceans, air, and land. This conclusion was based on her perception of what was, compared to what should have been, and led her to feelings that nothing really could be done, that it's too late, and that it's all hopeless. I always tell young people when they feel disillusioned that their sensitivity to hypocrisy may not be matched with a fully mature perspective that will come in a few years. In a sense, their intellect and perceptiveness is ahead of their perspective leading to feelings of hopelessness and disillusionment. When a young person understands where these feelings emerge from, they learn not to take the hopeless feelings so seriously and thus lessen the intensity of their pain.

Improved But Imperfect Reasoning. The logic of a 12 or 13 year old is more advanced than it was in earlier years. It is not, however, fully developed.

Adolescents now are able to discern alternatives, but they lack the experience and self-understanding to choose correctly. Caught in that tangle, they may simply act confused or choose inappropriately. Foolish choices may be as minor as wearing a spring jacket to school in a snowstorm. Or they may have potentially damaging results — driving too fast, choosing the wrong friends, abusing alcohol or drugs.

· Seemingly aware that their new skills of logic need sharpening, most adolescents will argue with little or no provocation. They will question rules, demand reasonable explanations of everything, and then respond with flawed counterarguments.

Identity and Emotional Development

Identity is defined as the ordering of one's various roles and characteristics; it implies a degree of self-awareness of personal traits, abilities, weaknesses, preferences and values.

Searching for an identity strikes many parents as a form of indulgence, an excuse for outrageous behavior. Examples are many from unusual hair styles, to distinct clothing styles, musical preferences, language, and videos. Today's parents, however, should keep in mind that today there are more choices for adolescents than ever before. Society's rules about sex roles are changing. No longer is it assumed that a girl will grow up to define herself solely as wife and mother; no longer is it assumed that a boy will grow up to take over his father's farm or business. Adolescents now juggle a much more complex set of societal expectations of how they should be. At the same time, society sends mixed signals to young people about what society values and expects. We tell young people to value education and knowledge, yet we idealize athletes and actors, not scientists and educators. The mass media depicts a multitude of alternative lifestyles, thereby making it increasingly tough for adolescents to know who they are, where they fit and where they're headed.

The adolescent drive to establish an identity arises in some part from those budding intellectual capacities discussed earlier. As an adolescent acts out the different ways to be, his or her behavior ranges from amusing to alarming.

The major signs of identity development are becoming self-conscious, alternating between independence and dependence, acting worried, anxious, and withdrawn.

Self-Consciousness. Most adolescents go through a period of self-absorption and narcissism. Seeing themselves as they believe others see them, they become deeply concerned about their inadequacies.

Psychologist David Elkind uses the term "imaginary audience" to describe the adolescent's notion that the whole world is focused on him or her. This perception contributes to many adolescents' assumptions that no one else has ever felt as they do. They become convinced that no one can understand their feelings and that everyone else is doing things better than they are.

Self-consciousness peaks in early adolescence and largely accounts for the obsessive concern with clothes and image at that time of life. Many young adolescents equate appearance and identity. Not knowing what he or she really thinks or how he or she really wants to act, the young adolescent experiments with eccentric clothes, hairstyles, gestures and slang. A negative response to these behaviors is usually counter-productive; it only convinces the teenager that the parent does not understand.

Adolescents will take teasing or derogatory remarks with profound seriousness — a seriousness that seems inconsistent with their intellectual growth in less personal matters. Relationships with siblings may also suffer during this vulnerable time.

Independence vs. Dependence. Adolescence is a tug-of-war between childhood and adulthood. Leaving childhood, the adolescent recognizes that he or she must give up one kind of freedom to gain another.

As a child, he or she was free to pursue immediate gratification while parents took care of most everything. As an adolescent, he or

11

she yearns for freedom to make choices without taking on the responsibilities of adulthood. Having a career, getting married, buying a house and car, raising and supporting children are parts of a dark, unknown future. Many adolescents feel overwhelmed at the prospect of these impending burdens, especially if parents have over-emphasized their negative aspects. The typical response is to become angry toward parents and other adults making demands.

The adolescent's push toward independence may involve some rebellion and challenge of accepted norms. By comparing parents' values to other possibilities, the adolescent asserts his or her own independence and learns more about choices, consequences, and his or her own identity.

Rebellion may also be used as a defense mechanism. Adolescents often do not have all the coping and communication skills that would help them to separate from their parents more effectively. As a result, they may resort to other ways of coping or communicating their desire to separate themselves. Thus the adolescent afraid of independence may create friction at home as a motivation to break away.

The degree and intensity of anger and rebellion vary greatly from adolescent to adolescent. Even in the calmest home, however, it is normal for boys to separate themselves from family activities. Girls tend to develop new emotional ties outside the family but are more apt to retain a close attachment with family concerns.

Worry, Anxiety and Withdrawal. Spending hours alone in their room, exhibiting frequent and abrupt mood swings, acting worried or anxious — all of these are common coping strategies used by adolescents.

It is important for parents to recognize that, from the adolescent perspective, stress abounds. The onset of puberty and the consequent anger at loss of childhood create internal instability. Parents may be coping with career changes, unemployment, or divorce. Corporate relocation, a disrupter of family life, is a reality for many of today's young. School provides ever increasing academic pressure and may also be the setting for stealing, fights, substance abuse, overt sexual activity, and competition for material status symbols. Social relationships meet new needs, but they come with a price: exclusion from cliques, prejudice, and betrayals of confidence.

In all these domains, the adolescent lacks experience. His or her performance in any of them may fail to meet personal expectations and the sense of self-esteem is apt to topple.

Sometimes adolescents can experience depression or anxiety related to performance demands. Their own or parents' standards that don't get met can result in feelings of failure that lead to depression or anxiety. Adolescents who experience depression or anxiety will often withdraw, sleep an excessive amount, or have difficulty with sleep patterns (experience difficulty going to sleep or waking up early). They may experience fatigue, have headaches unrelated to physical causes, feel apathetic or irritable, feel isolated or helpless, be obsessed with a problem or fear, engage in self-blame — self-downing, get angry quickly without warning, and experience increased difficulty communicating with family and friends.

If these symptoms present themselves and appear intense and or frequent, they may not be just a developmental moment, but may reflect more serious emotional issues requiring professional help.

In these — and in all — situations of "normally disturbed" behavior, the parents' best weapon is to remain calm and sympathetic. Let your teenager know that his or her problems are taken seriously and that he or she can talk about them without a lecture, unsolicited advice, or criticism from you. Avoid reacting to unprovoked and illogical outbursts of anger. Frequent mood swings and related problems are most common in early adolescence when identity is most fragile and peer groups have yet to fill the void.

Social and Sexual Development

Peer Relationships. When surveyed about their preferences concerning with whom to spend their free time, adolescents say they prefer their friends over family, classmates, other adults, and solitude.

Friends have several advantages. Friends can be chosen and dropped. They impose few limits and never ask that the laundry be done or impose curfews. Time spent with friends is recreational; time with adults usually involves unchosen demands.

The increased importance of peer relationships begins during early puberty. At this time, girls establish extremely close friendships with a few other girls. Boys, too establish close same-sex relationships, but typically on a less intimate basis. Girls are more likely to share secrets and talk on the phone; boys spend time together shooting baskets or playing video games.

Somewhere between ages 13 and 15, most adolescents broaden

this social circle to a peer group. (This can happen earlier when stability at home is lacking.) Peer groups fill a significant void for adolescents who are in the process of separating from a family.

The group usually includes boys and girls who party together or date each other and who tend to meet at the same hangout. The hangout is usually a neutral spot where the group is free from parental oversight.

Same-sex relationships are de-emphasized as attachments to the opposite sex grow stronger. Once close relationships between girls may become shallow and exploitative. Competitiveness between girls follows as they compete with each other for relationships with boys. Further, they become more competitive specific to dress, attractiveness, and who is in the most popular group or has the most popular or handsome boyfriend.

The peer group now becomes the standard-setter, determining standards of dress, attitudes toward parents, the importance of academic achievement, acceptable behavior toward the opposite sex, and use of drugs and alcohol. The mid-adolescent (14-15 year old) may behave like a blind conformist in his or her peer group and, at the same time, may maintain a feeling of uniqueness. He or she may also develop a close relationship with a non-custodial adult, thereby discovering more about alternative adult role models.

Through and in spite of all this, however, most adolescents will retain the values of their parents.

Sexual Relationships. At some point, usually during the mid-to-latter part of adolescence, many boys and girls develop exclusive relationships with the opposite sex. The path toward this milestone, however, begins much earlier, even before the physical evidence of puberty arrives.

Boy-girl parties now typically start in about sixth grade. At that age, though, the sexes tend to segregate themselves, even in the party setting. In young adolescence, in fact, same-sex relationships may still be so intense that they have sexual overtones.

Some young adolescents develop infatuations with unattainable persons, like a teacher.

Girls are more likely to develop an early romantic interest in a particular boy, but most of this early interaction is limited to talking about who likes whom. When true pairing off does occur, it usually happens in groups. The experience is more socially than sexually instructive. Outside of parties, most contact is maintained by phone or the passing of notes.

In some instances, young adolescents feel a vague guilt about their affection for a boyfriend or girlfriend, imagining that the amount of love they have to give is finite and must be subtracted from that they have given to their parents. Such feelings tend to escalate arguments and friction with parents; it is as though the child is aiming to prove the parents don't deserve all that much love anyway.

How adolescents respond to the early stages of their physical maturation varies. Studies show that boys seem to respond more positively than girls do. Boys feel proud; girls feel awkward. Both sexes become concerned about the size of their sexual organs. Young adolescent boys may also have some concerns about homosexuality.

By the time of mid-adolescence, more overt exploration of sexuality occurs. Most boys are easily aroused but fear loss of control. They may also feel tremendous pressure to know what to do and how to do it well.

Psychologists who work with adolescents note that problems with sexual dysfunction are appearing earlier. Some of the problems, they say, comes from the disappearance of standard markers that tell us how to behave. There was a time, for example, when a first-date kiss was unacceptable. That is no longer true and the adolescent pair on a first date are left with no external standard of appropriate behavior.

Romance and sexual experience are also fertile ground for adolescent disillusionment, especially for girls. The fantasy of romance as an ideal state is easily dashed by several factors — the realization that the loved one is flawed, the disapproval of people whose opinions are respected, and the failure of sex itself to live up to its advance billing.

Schoolwork and Motivation

Our society places a low value on the goods and services that adolescents are capable of providing. Achievement in school thus becomes a primary criterion for success and a vehicle for getting parental and social acceptance.

Academic achievement, however, does not come easily to everyone. Further, it requires delay of gratification and, for some, is not appealing. Disturbing but typical symptoms of academic pressure may include many things:

- An academically bad year is not uncommon. The young

15

adolescent may break a pattern of good performance and become sloppy in his or her work, especially in those least favorite subjects.

• Girls' grades in English and arts classes may improve while science and math grades drop. The opposite is true for boys. The reason? Many believe it is a matter of cultural conditioning. Some studies have shown that symptoms of depression in girls actually lessen as their grades in so-called "masculine" subjects fall.

• Many adolescents become highly critical of their teachers. Few will accept the ideas that algebra will make them better film makers or that future engineers should be familiar with Shakespeare. Teachers who lack enthusiasm and who feel threatened rank the lowest by their adolescent students.

• Adolescents begin to think seriously about vocational alternatives; goals, however, change frequently. They also tend to simplify what is involved in achieving career goals.

Drug and Alcohol Use

The line of demarcation between developmentally normal and abnormal use of alcohol and drugs is vague at best. That vagueness is an indication of a society-wide lack of consensus on the subject. Many parents of today's teens, for example, experimented with drugs as part of the political activism of the late 1960s and early 1970s. For some, part of the legacy of that era is the view that marijuana is a recreational drug; its use is barely a misdemeanor.

The use of drugs and alcohol today may begin as early as ages 11 and 12. Adolescents often find that marijuana is as readily available as alcohol; they know its effects are similar.

By mid-to-late adolescence, most will experiment with alcohol and marijuana out of curiosity or peer pressure or a combination of both. Parents' main concern should focus on keeping the communication channels open; adolescents should feel open to talk about these experiences and explorations. Parents can then convey the message that some forms of experimentation might be more tolerable when the adolescent is a bit older.

Probably the most difficult time for a parent when their teenager explores alcohol or drugs is knowing where to draw the line. By drawing the line, a parent indicates that something that their teen is doing will not be tolerated and will be dealt with. This is a step beyond just sharing values and letting a young person know how

16

the parent feels and where the parent stands regarding alcohol or drug use. A line should be drawn when use has become more than occasional, has begun to impair the adolescent's relationship at home, his or her functioning at school and at work, and has begun to change in hurtful ways their values and moral judgment. Families will draw lines that reflect their own values and behavior; each line will be different among families. Many parents will be more tolerant because of their own behavior with alcohol or drug exploration and occasional use. Other parents, because of their values, may find any exploration difficult to tolerate. However, these parents must remind themselves that, as part of adolescence in this particular society, exploration seems to be part of the territory.

Adolescent Characteristics

These are some of the ways teenagers act during adolescence. Some teenagers experience these characteristics earlier or later than their peers. Also the intensity and/or frequency of these characteristics may vary among teenagers.

- Become very self absorbed and narcissistic, to the exclusion of being able to show significant concern for parents' pain and dilemmas.

- Often feel that no one else has ever felt as they do and that no one can understand their feelings.

- Often equate clothes, appearance, and identity.

- Often prefer spending free time with friends instead of family.

- Become aware of appearance and clothes, spend a lot of time in front of the mirror and want clothing that is in style.

- Become quite self-conscious about body and looks (over- or under-weight, height, acne, size of feet, hands, and nose and eyes).

- Begin thinking of vocational interests, but these change frequently.

- Attitudes toward social, religious, ethics and racial values emerge and can differ with those of the parents.

- Cannot tolerate teasing or derogatory remarks; react adversely.

- Become overly critical about parents, siblings, and home; want the manners and dress of their family to be above average to impress their friends.

- Develop a "hangout". Feel that school is less a place of learning and more a place to see and be seen.

- Feel the need to rebel to achieve independence, (this can be very overt and include acting out or be more covert and involve more subtle rebelliousness).

- Shut parents out — more reluctant to talk to parents about school,

friends, emotions, want to figure
things out on their own.

• Spend much time alone, possibly
in their room.

• Begin blaming others (especially
family members) for their difficulty.

• May experiment with drugs,
alcohol and cigarettes.

• May idealize any adult (other than
their own parents), especially
other friends' parents, or may
see all adults as nonunderstanding
enemies.

Parents take heed. Most of what is described in this chapter is developmental — young people passing through an era. Knowing about this stage in their life protects you and them. You can say to yourself those helpful coping statements *"This is developmental and not personal."* You may not always like what you experience in the unfolding of your teen during adolescence, but it is helpful to know so much of what a parent experiences is supposed to be.

Chapter 3

Acting Out Behaviors

Make a mental list of your worst fears about your adolescent.

Do they include drugs? Alcohol? Sexual promiscuity? Any poor judgment that can cause physical or emotional damage?

If so, join the club. These are the most common worst fears for most parents of adolescents. All are examples of "acting-out" behaviors — things kids do that reflect the way kids feel.

During adolescence, young people find both direct and indirect ways of acting out their anger and upheaval. The direct ways include drinking, driving while drunk, taking drugs, dressing provocatively, verbally abusing parents, blatantly refusing to comply with parental requests. The indirect ways are quieter: doing poorly in school, dressing a little differently from the way mom and dad would like, subtly refusing to comply with parental requests, associating with people parents find distasteful, rejecting religious values dear to the family, and refusing to share information.

Some acting out is part of the developmental process; it is going to happen. Parents can keep it from escalating by better controlling their reactions. The byword is *cope* — don't react.

21

Before one of these acting-out situations presents itself, you can decide that you are not going to overreact. See yourself being calm and concerned rather than angry and out of control. Picture yourself handling a situation when your teenager does something that you don't like.

If your response to an acting-out episode is you being angry and yelling and screaming, being verbally aggressive, verbally attacking the kid, or bringing up past mistakes in a hurtful manner, chances are that your child is going to react to your anger. In the middle of everyone's anger, the important issues will get lost.

Your real job as a parent confronted with acting-out behaviors is to get to the heart of the matter.

A kid acting out is a kid trying to say something.

The kid's behavior is a communications tool — not a very good one, true, but it is an attempt at communicating. There will be plenty of time to respond to the episode with some kind of appropriate consequences. First, try to understand what is really going on.

Sometimes that is tough to do. Sometimes it is not.

Usually, anger is the trigger for an acting-out behavior. The root of that anger is often some kind of hurt. The parent facing an acting-out incident should try to find the anger and hurt beneath the surface. Sometimes all you have to do is ask.

"What happened? Why are you so upset?"

Sometimes caring questions can spark a discussion that gets to the source. Sometimes the fact that you are asking and that you care will surprise an adolescent into talking about it.

Some acting out is normal — part of the process of separation from family and development of an identity. Some acting out is not.

When the adolescent's emotional or physical health is threatened, when the ability to function is impaired, then we have passed beyond what is normal. Help is needed.

If you are seeing very intense episodes or very frequent episodes of acting-out behavior, then your teen's problems may be more serious than you realize. This is the time to seek some professional help. It is always better to err on the side of caution in these matters; if you suspect a serious problem, then contact a professional. He or she will give you some input on the present situation and perhaps some guidance on handling future situations.

Some kinds of acting-out behaviors grab parental attention more than others. Some behavior, such as very belligerent acts of noncompliance, prompt swift reactions. Examples of acting out can take many different forms during adolescence. Loud, overt acting out can take the form of sneaking out of the house in the middle of the night, breaking curfews, belligerently refusing to do what parents ask, being sexually promiscuous, going places that parents have forbidden them to go, associating with certain peers who elicit strong, negative feelings by parents, engaging in alcohol or drug use, and dressing in provocative ways that conflict with the parent's values. Less overt and more low-keyed ways of acting out often include not expressing one's potential in school or in sports, agreeing to do things that the parents have asked and then "forgetting", and nicely being unresponsive to parental expectations.

One behavior to which many parents do not respond (largely because of fear) is the suicide signal — the verbal suicide threat or gesture. This is an especially difficult behavior for parents. We are very uncomfortable talking about it.

But talking about it is the key — the crucial step. The immediate response to a suicide signal should be a parent's attempt to talk about the signal with the teen. Even the most subtle comment merits discussion. The gravest parental error in this situation is denial: refusal to recognize the suicide signal and talk about it.

When talking starts, it is important for the parent to try to understand the young person's feelings and pain rather than to try to talk him or her out of the pain. This is not a moment for problem solving; this is a moment to find understanding.

Those who deal with suicide tell us that most young people who have committed suicide spoke about it before they did it. If your adolescent is talking about suicide, find a professional who can help you evaluate the situation. Thoughts of suicide are not uncommon for adolescents and adults. However, in adolescence especially, the potential for danger exists. The professional can help parents determine if the danger is real and figure out what the signals mean. Knowing what the signals mean is a major help in knowing how to cope with them.

Some exploration of alcohol and drug use by many young people is to be expected during adolescence. There is, however, a difference between exploration and dependency or abuse. Parents must be alert to that threshold. Dabbling in something becomes abuse when a person's ability to function begins to deteriorate.

When does exploration end and abuse begin? Parents should be aware of several significant signals that may indicate their child is experiencing a problem with alcohol or drugs.

Signals That May Indicate Alcohol Or Drug Abuse

Your Adolescent:

• No longer obeys curfews or other basic house rules.

• Has changed friends significantly for the worst.

• Has begun skipping school consistently.

• Seems to be a different person.

• Has become abusive with parents, brothers, or sisters.

• Has begun stealing from family members.

• Has begun a "motel existence" within the house.

• Avoids involvement with other family members at all costs.

• Has been kicked out of school or fired from jobs more that once.

• Has changed his daily living habits dramatically.

Parents need to watch for signs of that deterioration, in school, at home, or on the job. Add up the signals and see what you've got. if grades are dropping and the adolescent is less responsible at home and you've seen some signs of alcohol or drug use — that adds up. What you may have is regular substance use and abuse and it is time for professional help. Too often, it is temptingly easy for parents to simply ignore the signs, to deny the problem. That denial only postpones the moment of confronting the problem and the task of getting help.

Another common arena for acting-out behavior is sexual. In this age of sexually transmitted diseases it is more important than ever for parents and teens to talk openly about sexual issues. As a parent trying to discuss these issues with a teen, you must remember the big difference between condoning and accepting. Accepting the fact that your young person may behave in a way you disagree with does not mean you condone that young person's behavior. You can do one without the other. You can help your young person to be responsible and still not agree with what he or she is doing.

An example is due. Your young person may be committed to a sexual relationship and you know about it and you have a choice. You can condemn and forbid or you can explore the decision and accept the reality of the decision. Without condoning the decision, you can help your young person be informed and responsible about its implications.

You can also let your children know where you stand on matters of sexual behavior and alcohol or drug use. Tell them what your values are. More important, show them. *Your behavior must reflect your beliefs or you lose all credibility with your teenager.* Young people are quick to spot hypocrisy.

Talking To Your Teenager About Sex

- Be clear about your own feelings. Think ahead about what you want to say about your own beliefs and attitudes.

- Separate your teen from his or her behavior. If he or she has done something sexually with which you don't agree, do not reject him or her as a person while you disagree with what he or she did.

- Remember: if you are critical and nonsupportive, your young person will learn to tune you out or will not share openly about sexual issues.

- Reassure your teenager, especially when the teen is experiencing sexual issues for the first time, that he or she is normal.

- Be aware that your attitudes and feelings may be conveyed nonverbally through facial expressions, tone of voice, gestures, and silence.

- Share your values with your children by providing them with guidelines in making choices.

- Don't be put off by your teen's embarrassment when discussing sexuality. Be understanding, and gently share your own understandings even if your teen rolls his or her eyes saying "I already know that stuff."

- Ask questions to understand, not to show them they are wrong.

- Don't feel a need to be an expert. If you don't know something admit it and find further information.

Adapted from Planned Parenthood's
Helpful Hints On How To Talk With Your Child About Sexuality.

It all comes back to talking with one another. The more you know about your teenager's behavior, the greater the impact you can have on his or her choices. You cannot control those choices; you can only affect them. (Usually, too, the reality of what the kid is doing is not nearly as scary as what you imagined him or her doing.)

Sometimes parents say they'd rather not know what their teen is doing away from home. Ignorance is bliss — that kind of thing.

That brand of ignorance may be comforting in the short run. In the long haul, though, it is no good. You need the knowledge to help the kid make choices, to aid your own ability to cope, to head off unpleasant surprises in the future.

Once again, keeping perspective becomes critical. Perspective helps you avoid over reacting. One adolescent is already acting out. What these episodes do not need is a second adolescent — this one wrapped in an adult body — acting out in retaliation. The goal is to help the teenager learn to make better choices.

When acting out behaviors becomes very hurtful or very frequent or very intense, or when they inhibit your child's ability to function with others, read the signals. That is the time for professional assistance. Get it.

Chapter 4

Making Honesty And Openness Safe

Ask other parents what type of relationship they would most like to have with their teenagers. Chances are most will tell you they want a relationship that is open and honest.

Well, you say, what do you mean by that? And they tell you that they want their teenagers to be able to come to them with any concern. Anything at all. In turn, they want to be able to get an honest answer from their teenager to such key questions as, "Where are you going? Who is going along?"

Openness and honesty. That's what they want at the foundation of the relationship. That's the ticket.

Like all tickets, it has a price. Such a relationship can be achieved, but only with parents willing to pay the price. The price is an obligation to encourage and reinforce honesty. Sounds easy, doesn't it? Think a moment longer.

What this means is that a parent is obligated to appreciate the *process* of open and honest sharing more than the *content* of what is being shared. Your appreciation of your teenager's honest openness is greater than your reaction to the news being shared.

This does not mean you are giving up your feelings and values — or your right to express them. It does mean that if you don't learn to value the process of open sharing, then you are likely to overreact to the information you are hearing. Once your teenager knows you may overreact, he or she quickly learns to edit. The adolescent will become very careful about what information can be shared openly and what information has to be avoided or covered with a lie.

There are many examples of teenagers choosing not to share with their parents in critical areas. These include sharing about sexual exploration, alcohol or drug use, traveling to a different part of the city which is forbidden, experiencing feelings of hurt or rejection in a relationship, doing poorly on a test in school, having a conflict with the teacher, no longer feeling the same connections to religious values, and the list goes on.

Adolescence is a time when many difficult issues arise. *From us, as parents, our children learn what is safe to communicate and what is not.* If we cannot communicate, how can we work on the difficult issues?

In the climate of concern today about drinking and driving, many parents and their teens have worked out contracts dealing with this issue. Typically, they go like this: When the adolescent has had too much to drink, he or she can call a parent and know that parent will come to pick up the adolescent and drive him or her safely home. This contract is based upon one critical requirement: once the young person calls, the parent will not respond with a lecture, a lot of flack, a bundle of grief. Without that stipulation tied into the contract, few kids would make this essential call. The kid can do it because he or she knows the honesty will be respected. It is safe.

So in the face of an open sharing relationship, are parents powerless when they come up against behaviors they don't like?

Not at all. If the relationship is an honest and open one, then parents can throw in their two cents. As the teen can openly share his or her feelings, so can the parent. The goal is to help the teen work through the thorns of an issue.

The adolescent will sometimes make the choices you like, sometimes not. If the natural and logical consequences of the teenager's choices are not pleasant, the teenager will, like the rest of us, probably modify his or her thinking on this issue. That is a process we all go through. Parents help their adolescent through it by providing an adult perspective which includes the parents' experiences including mistakes, errors in judgment, painful consequences, and their observations of others in similar circumstances. Only when the parent-teen relationship is an open and honest one does that perspective stand a chance of being heard.

The prerequisite to honest and open sharing is the feeling of safety.

Feeling safe is knowing that the person you are confiding in will not reject you as a person — even if he or she strongly disagrees with your point of view. That is something we treasure as adults. It is something we must recognize as parents.

Our young people may share with us information or beliefs or actions we find most unpleasant. We can dislike the information and the beliefs and the actions but we must continue to accept and love the person. Only then will they feel safe enough to share with honesty and openness.

Encouraging honesty and openness requires some parental restraint. The parent who wants this to work must take the time to listen before asking questions or sharing personal opinions. **Parents who choose to listen are always more influential in their adolescents' lives and more informed of their adolescents' activities than are those parents who choose not to listen.**

The bottom line is this: **The news will not always be good.**

Young people going through adolescence will not always reflect their family's values — BUT — nurturing honest and open communication is one of the best ways parents can help their teens through this period of development.

One word about realistic expectations: do not expect or demand total openness. Even if you diligently follow all the recommendations, do not expect total honesty. Sometimes your adolescent will choose to withhold some information — even if he or she knows it is safe to share with you. That, too, is part of the developmental process.

Adolescence is a process that requires increased separation from family. It is a time for creating one's own identity. That means it is necessary to pull away, to keep some things private. It is a necessary and often positive part of the process that some child-to-parent sharing be limited. The wise parent will not overreact.

Recognize the reality by recalling your own adolescence. Recall those actions and feelings and beliefs you explored but chose not to talk about with your mom or dad.

Recognizing and accepting the process of teenagers separating and forging their own identities is the antidote to parental overreaction. When parental overreaction and demanding are absent, the atmosphere is ripe for safe and trusting sharing between parent and teen.

Chapter 5

Parental Anger

Are you a parent?

Then you will get angry. Sometimes — no matter how controlled you are — your children are going to do things to which you will react with anger. It happens to all of us.

We can, by learning something about our anger, perhaps make it flare less often, less intensely, and for a shorter period of time. What we are looking for here is not perfect control (that hasn't been invented yet), but a way to damper our reactions to the things those kids do.

Anger can be healthy or unhealthy. The healthy kind stays at the level of irritation, annoyance, aggravation. The unhealthy kind turns hurtful: rage, angry shouting, words or fists thrown to humiliate and cause pain.

As part of their development, teenagers are bound to do some things — probably many things — that are difficult for parents to cope with.

For example, he says he's going to the library, and he ends up at the mall arcade instead. Or she says her science project is finished, but she has yet to pick a subject.

You get upset. That is okay. But you need to get upset at the level of healthy anger — irritated, annoyed, aggravated. When you keep your upset at that level, you are able to choose your responses. If you let it rise higher, you lose control and choice. Maintaining anger at a healthy level means that you can react in a way that may teach something to your teenager.

The capacity for anger inside each of us deserves some closer examination. It is there. Where does it come from?

Just about always it comes from expectations. We all have views of what *should, ought to, must be.* We all have views of how our kid *should, ought to , must* act. When the kid's actions don't match the expectations, parental anger is pretty apt to happen.

When we set the expectations too high, make them unrealistic, we are setting the kid up for failure to measure up and setting ourselves up for anger.

What we say to ourselves (or don't say to ourselves) can have a lot to do with how upset or angry we become.

"I can't stand it! I just can't stand it!"

Schroeder used to say that about Lucy's visions of their future wedded bliss in the "Peanuts" comic strip. But he could stand it; her comments were tolerable and he survived.

Your teenager's refusal to obey you is something you can stand. That doesn't mean you can't apply consequences for disobedience. You can. But you also can stand the fact of his or her disobedience.

Know that and you will be better able to cope. Being able to stand difficult things is called frustration tolerance. To have low frustration tolerance when you believe you "can't stand" certain difficult situations is one of the big roadblocks to your ability to cope.

So is the act of applying "big-deal" labels to situations. When you tell yourself that this last trick your teen pulled is "just awful," "the most terrible thing you can imagine," or "devastating," you are prodding yourself into overreaction.

Imagine the potential response by the parent when the teen wrecks the car for the first time or comes home drunk for the first time or doesn't study for a test and makes significantly lower grades than ever before, or gets caught in a lie when he or she is supposed to be one place and is somewhere else, doing something he or she was not supposed to do. In each instance, the parent decides whether this is catastrophic, awful and terrible, or something that occasionally accompanies the territory of dealing with an adolescent, that deserves a response and possibly consequences, but does not deserve the big-deal label.

Sometimes parental anger comes from the mistaken notion that our adolescent's misbehavior is a clear sign that we are bad parents.

When you believe that — and you let your child know you belive that — the scene is set:

"You'd better behave, because if you don't, then I'm bad, and if you make me look like a bad parent, I am going to be really, really mad — and you're going to pay!"

Some among us believe that anger is a tool of discipline, that our teenagers will listen to us only when we show them our anger. So we use it to get their attention. However, we can get attention by being clear and firm in our sharing our views, values, and consequences that are appropriate at the time.

So much for the sources of parental anger. It is going to show up. What can we do to make it less hurtful for everyone concerned?

We can start by talking to ourselves, by carefully defining our own feelings. Anger is often tied to demands. "I demand that this child get good grades," "I demand his obedience."

See the potential for anger lessen when you get rid of the word and the feeling of demand. Replace "I demand" with "I prefer" or "I want." Say to *yourself*, "I want him to obey," "I prefer that she get good grades." Presto! Your view of your teenager's behavior has suddenly become more reasonable and less unattainable. And you are less prone to the angry overreaction.

It is normal for kids to be difficult in certain ways at certain times in their development. Knowing what is normal at a certain step will make you more comfortable and relaxed as a parent. And you will be able to send yourself one of the best "self-statements" possible: "What that kid is doing now is not exactly pleasant, but it is something to be expected somewhere along the way."

Being able to tell yourself may not make you happy with the kid's behavior, but it will make you better able to cope with the situation.

Another thing to remind yourself of from time to time: there is a difference between what you can't stand and what you don't like. Being able to tell yourself, "I don't like this but I can stand it" helps you manage your anger and cope with the difficulty.

Keeping things in perspective is a challenge — but it is essential to coping with parental anger. Perspective is built by choice. Instead of using those "awful" and "terrible" labels as you look at your teen's misbehavior, choose some perspective-building adjectives: "unfortunate", "too bad", "inconvenient", "regrettable", "a real pain." The evidence is there: **people who are able to maintain perspective, experience much less emotional upset.**

To keep healthy anger from escalating into hurtful anger requires a watchful eye. You need to be aware that the healthy level of irritation and annoyance has the potential to turn hurtful.

It helps to recognize which annoying teenage misbehaviors are most likely to set you up. What does your adolescent do that you really react to with your own craziness? When you see that one coming — and sometimes there is a warning — you can prepare yourself. Say to yourself, "I don't do well with this behavior; I'd better prepare not to overreact."

There are some other things you can say to yourself in moments of teenage misbehavior that may be helpful to you. These are the day-to-day weapons you can use to maintain your power over your anger, to keep it at a healthy level.

Try saying these to yourself. You will find them more helpful than some of the messages you've been sending inside.

1. My adolescent **will** misbehave — sometimes more than other times. This is highly probable.
2. When my teenager misbehaves, he or she has only broken a rule. Period! This does **not** mean I am a bad parent or person unless I allow it to mean that.
3. When my teenager misbehaves, I can teach him or her something by (a.) providing a meaningful penalty (without anger) and (b.) later giving recognition to acceptable behavior.
4. My kids will make mistakes even if they know the rules.
5. It is unfortunate when my kid misbehaves, but it is not a disaster.
6. It is not pleasant when my adolescent misbehaves, but it is tolerable.
7. It is preferable that my kids behave, but it is probable that they won't all the time and I can tolerate that.
8. I do not have to get angry to discipline my teenager. If I find myself yelling or repeating warnings, I am not using an effective discipline technique and I should probably rethink my strategy in this and similar situations.
9. Sometimes I will get angry because I am a fallible human being and I sometimes set myself up with unrealistic thoughts about my kid's behavior.

Parental anger can be helpful anger. When it is helpful, it allows parents to share their feelings in an assertive manner. Sharing assertively means directing comments to the teenager's behavior rather than to the teenager as a person. You can be helpful when you let the teenager know how you feel and what you want, when you stay on the issue at hand, when you avoid verbal abuse and personal attack.

Hurtful anger can lead to parental aggression. That aggression moves quickly to attack on the teenager as a person. The attacks may come as yelling, ridicule, severe sarcasm, or perhaps the parent's withdrawal from the adolescent as a type of emotional punishment. The reaction to any of these from a teenager? Perhaps an angry outburst in retaliation, perhaps anger turned inward, perhaps loss of self-worth, or perhaps deep depression.

Adolescents need to hear feedback from their parents. They need to know how you feel and what you expect. Parental anger clouds the message. The teenager is more likely to react to the anger than to the message. So, nothing is communicated.

Anger is not a synonym for caring. You do not show how concerned you are by flying into a rage. What you do show is that you are unable to manage your own emotions. A parent can care deeply and still respond in a matter-of-fact manner.

Now then, none of us will maintain that matter-of-fact response at all times. I can remember with my oldest son asking him to help me cut the grass and having him turn to me and say, "I don't have to do what you say and there is nothing you can do about it." I felt the flash of anger and I confronted him, grabbing him physically in the garage, pushing him and angrily saying to him, "You will not talk to me that way and if I ask you to do something you will do it." Then he reacted to my angry emotional response. Clearly it was appropriate for me to confront his refusal; however, remembering that he was going through a specific oppositional moment in adolescence would have allowed me to approach this situation a little less emotionally. If I had been less reactive he would have quickly come around to doing what I asked with possibly a brief delay in order for him to feel some control in this situation. We will slip up. Parents are wonderful, fallible human beings. Just like their kids. Every now and then, the best-meaning among us will fly off the handle, say things to our adolescent we don't mean, get hurtful.

Then comes the rush of guilt and remorse and the possibility of a real attack upon our own self-worth. This is when we are apt to say, "What a lousy parent I am — what a low-life, what a crummy person..."

Hold it right there!

As you try to be careful to separate what your child does from who your child is, so should you work at the same separation of perform-ance from self on you. From time to time you will probably do something unfortunate or regrettable as a parent. You will attack the kid rather than his performance on the biology test. Recognize that as simply an inadequate act on your part at that moment. No life sentence is involved.

If you fall into the habit of generalizing about yourself as a bad parent or person, you will be more likely to turn in another poor performance. Getting down on yourself will not make you perform better as a parent.

So — stop the self-punishment. Instead, understand that what you did needs correcting, and consider how you might have acted differently, how you will try to respond next time something similar comes up. And, while you are at it, let the teenager know that you didn't handle things so well there and you're sorry about that.

Wait until you have your emotions under control, then try some-thing like this:

"What you did was not okay with me, but I made myself upset about it and I am sorry I yelled at you."

In your apology, you are setting an example and we all know that parental example is still one of the primary ways kids learn. Your apology has shown the teenager that errors are made and admitting them is an okay thing to do.

You are always a model for your child's method of dealing with the world. By watching and listening to you use helpful rather than hurtful anger, he and she learn some of those coping skills themselves.

As a model, you need to let your kids hear the "self-talk" that goes on as you are expressing your helpful brand of anger. (We just about always let them hear the "you-bum-you" kind of self-talk associated with hurtful anger.)

Reveal your thoughts and feelings at the moment of the anger-provoking incident. Say, for example, that you catch your 13-year-old puffing away on a cigarette in the basement. Here's what you might say out loud so that the 13-year-old has a chance to get the full and clear message:

"I know that you may be curious about smoking. But it is not okay with Mom and me that you smoke — even though we understand your curiosity. I don't like you trying this — cigarettes are unhealthy — but I do realize you are going to be curious. I don't like it, but I can stand it. There will, however be some serious consequences if the smoking continues."

That is admittedly a mouthful. But you can see that the 13-year-old will have a clear idea of how his father feels, how he is controlling his anger, how he intends to provide consequences for continued behavior of this kind. And the young teen may discover from this a method he can use to control his own angry responses. We can hope.

If it comes to pass, if you do catch your teenager handling a difficult situation well, encourage that response. When you witness your adolescent walk away rather than confront, express annoyance rather than rage, imitate your verbal "self-statements," take time to reinforce the behavior:

"You handled that well — I'm proud of how you dealt with this."

Only a few words — but words important even to an adolescent.

What about hurtful anger that has already slipped out? Can it be controlled once out of the bag?

Yes, it can. The key thing here is interrupting the process of rising anger. Different techniques work for different people.

For some, leaving the scene and doing something energy-consuming will do the trick. Walking, running, lifting weights, doing aerobics — all are anger burners for some people. Others turn to relaxing techniques such as music, the hot tub, a good book or magazine, a movie to reduce the upset. Even counting backwards from 100 can help lessen the anger of the moment.

Sometimes the STOP-THINK method works wonders in breaking that chain of escalating anger. **Yell** inside yourself those two words: STOP-THINK. Disrupt the chain of hurtful, angry thoughts. Then do it. Stop and think about how you are making yourself angry. What are you saying to yourself about your teenager's misbehavior that is making you so upset? How would you prefer to be acting?

You can choose. Close your eyes and picture yourself acting in that preferred way. See yourself calmer and you will begin to feel calmer.

By now, the message should be clear: hurtful anger gets in the way of parent-teen relationships. It sets up resentment in the teen. The resentment can take some very unpleasant forms — hostile withdrawal, intentional forgetfulness, quiet destruction.

Hurtful anger also robs both parent and teenager of the warm, nurturing feelings that enrich both lives. It makes honesty between parent and teen impossible.

Sometimes the news a teenager has is not good news. He or she knows hurtful anger is a probable parental reaction, honesty is out of the question. It is too dangerous. The teen learns to tell you what you want to hear, what is safe to tell.

Finally, hurtful anger is a great producer of parental guilt. Guilt is really nothing more or less than anger turned inward. It paves the way for you to attack your own worth and feel more resentment toward the kid who "caused you" to feel so bad in the first place.

Helpful anger, on the other hand, opens the door to honesty in parent-adolescent relationships. Guilt and resentment leave; safety and honesty enter.

The teenager feels safe in self-expressions. He or she does not have to guard comments and feelings. And the relationship with the parent will be one both more genuine and more significant.

Chapter 6

Managing Parental Anger

Recognizing Hurtful And Helpful Thoughts

It may be helpful for you to make a list of situations which keep happening — starting with those often associated with full-blown anger. You can then begin working with the mild anger situations and gradually move on to more difficult situations using these techniques.

Learning to recognize non-helpful thoughts and to change them to helpful thoughts will assist me to become a more effective parent **before** the situation again arises, **during** an anger-breeding situation, and **after** I have made myself angry.

Using Self-Help Worksheets
During And After Angry Situations.

Several self-help worksheets with challenging situations that occur with adolescents are included. The situations covered are examples of situations that are often difficult for parents to handle. By reviewing and using these self-help sheets, you can become better at identifying both your non-helpful thoughts and more helpful thoughts. By following the step-by-step self-help sheet instructions, you can improve your ability to deal with anger.

The self-help worksheets can offer you a tool to analyze situations that have already been hard to handle. So the next time a similar situation arises you will be able to manage it more successfully. The self-help worksheets also will provide you **during** a difficult situation some help in managing it by having examples of non-helpful and helpful thoughts for you to immediately review.

Using self-help worksheets before or during an anger-breeding situation:

To use the self-help worksheet before or during anger-breeding situations, go to a quiet place to review the self-help form (do not attempt to review while remaining in the anger-breeding situation). Look at the self-help worksheet and begin.

A. Identify the situation or what may happen (1).
B. Identify your feelings (3) and how you behave or feel like behaving (4).
C. Identify thoughts to yourself that do not help you handle the situation better (2).
D. Identify what you can think to yourself to help you handle the situation better (5).
E. Identify how you will feel (6) and how you will behave (7), if you begin to think more helpfully.
F. Identify discipline strategies/alternative parent behavior options for handling the situation.

Using self-help worksheets following an anger-breeding situation:

A. Identify the situation or what happened (1).
B Identify how you felt (3) and what your behavior looked like (4).
C. Identify what you thought to yourself that did **not** help you handle the situation (2) and led to how you felt (3).
D. Identify what you can think to yourself to help you handle the situation better (5).
E. Identify how you can feel (6) and what your behavior can look like (7) if you think more helpfully.
F. Identify discipline strategies/alternative parent behavior options for handling the situation.

Self-Help Worksheet for Managing Parental Anger

1. What happened/the situation.

2. What I thought to myself that did *not* help me handle the situation.

3. How I felt.

4. What my behavior looked like.

5. What I can think to myself to help me handle the situation better.

6. How I can feel.

7. What my behavior can look like.

8. Discipline strategies/alternative parent behavior options for handling the situation.

Self-Help Worksheet for Managing Parental Anger: Teenage Example

1. **What happened/the situation.**
   My child continually says he has no homework and at the parent-teacher meeting I was told my child will always have some homework.

2. **What I thought to myself that did not help me handle the situation.**
   How dare he lie to me! He must think I'm stupid and he can get away with this. He should know this is hurting him and is irresponsible. What must the teacher think of me?

3. **How I felt.**
   Angry
   Worried
   Frustrated
   Embarrassed

4. **What my behavior looked like.**
   Argumentative
   Confrontive
   Cutting down the child as a person
   Overly punitive

5. **What I can think to myself to help me handle the situation better.**
   Sometimes kids take the easy way out and are not truthful about their homework. Not all kids at this age are self-motivated and disciplined. Many kids at this age don't see past today. Not doing his homework does not make me a bad parent.

6. **How I can feel.**
   Concerned

7. **What my behavior can look like.**
   Educative, firm but patient, encouraging

8. **Discipline strategies/alternative parent behavior options for handling the situation.**
   I can set up with my child a regular study time whether or not he has homework. I can request a weekly progress report from school until he is consistently on track. I can request a teacher conference with my child to make him aware that his choices are affecting his grades. I can work out a reward/contract with my child to encourage him to complete his work and turn it in. I can provide a punishment of limited duration so that it makes a point of disapproval and provides a consequence that does not leave the teen feeling hopelessly limited and rebellious.

Self-Help Worksheet for Managing Parental Anger: Teenage Example

1. **What happened/the situation.**
   I let my son use the family car and he came home without the gas cap.

2. **What I thought to myself that did not help me handle the situation.**
   What a screw-up! Can't you take care of anything! I can't stand it when I give you a privilege and you abuse it!

3. **How I felt.**
   Angry
   Intolerant of frustration

4. **What my behavior looked like.**
   Yelled and screamed
   Grounded him for 6 months

5. **What I can think to myself to help me handle the situation better.**
   Anyone can lose a gas cap. Just because he screwed up doesn't make him a screw-up. This won't be the first or last time he makes a mistake. I want to get the responsibility issue across, not my anger.

6. **How I can feel.**
   Annoyed

7. **What my behavior can look like.**
   Firm
   Matter-of-fact

8. **Discipline strategies/alternative parent behavior options for handling the situation.**
   I can help him recreate his activities to help him figure out where he may have left it and then help him track it down and get it. If it's lost, I can have him price a new one and purchase it with his money.

Self-Help Worksheet for Managing Parental Anger: Teenage Example

1. **What happened/the situation.**
   My daughter went out and promised to be home on time. She came home 1 hour late.

2. **What I thought to myself that did not help me handle the situation.**
   How dare she defy me. I won't stand for this. She should always be home on time. What if something happened to her? What if she was in an accident?

3. **How I felt.**
   Angry
   Worried

4. **What my behavior looked like.**
   Yelled and screamed
   Grounded her for a long period of time

5. **What I can think to myself to help me handle the situation better.**
   Sometimes lateness is unavoidable; I want her to know how to handle it. It's unacceptable to be late. She made a judgment error, but she's not a bad person. I don't want this to become a pattern.

6. **How I can feel.**
   Annoyed and concerned

7. **What my behavior can look like.**
   Firm

8. **Discipline strategies/alternative parent behavior options for handling the situation.**
   I can let her know this is not acceptable and won't be condoned by restricting the privilege for a time. If it was unavoidable, I want her to know how to handle it so I won't worry myself.

46

Chapter 7

Hearing Feelings Effectively:
Don't Forget To Listen

One of the most frustrating aspects of being an adolescent is the risky business of sharing one's feelings with one's parents. Such sharings often conclude with the adolescent walking away feeling completely unheard and misunderstood.

Most teens are not gluttons for being misunderstood and not heard. It takes only a few of these occasions for the typical teenager to say, "Forget it, what's the point?" End of attempts at sharing.

What goes wrong here?

The most common parental error is a well-meaning one. It just doesn't work well.

Many times a parent becomes so intent on solving the problem or sharing some adult wisdom that he or she forgets to listen. At least, so it seems to the adolescent. No evidence is given that the parent has heard or understood the feelings shared.

Now, this typical parent response usually springs from caring and from the heartfelt desire to make things better for the child. But that is not how it comes off. From the young person the common reaction is "Mom/Dad doesn't understand me and that makes me mad," and none of that valuable adult advice/wisdom/problem-solving gets heard.

47

If a brother or sister is around, they get the same message: "They didn't hear Bubba and they won't hear me and I'm sure not going to risk telling them anything important."

The goal then, is for the parent to make the young person feel that he or she is heard and understood. Rather than try to change the feelings a young person is sharing, the parent needs to try to first hear and understand him or her. That is what empathy is — the attempt to appreciate and understand another's feelings, to walk in another's moccasins.

This is a process most difficult when the shared feelings are painful ones — either to the child or to the parent. But empathy is a known powerful medicine, especially when feelings are painful. The child doing the sharing can see that the parent is trying to understand. The recognition that "I am being heard" is a powerful healer.

We have said it before — and probably will again — adolescents are individuals, each is one of a kind. Parents trying to empathize will be more successful if they remember that and honor the uniqueness of this child's feelings and ideas.

It can be a big hurdle to climb. But once the adolescent feels that he or she is being understood and that he or she has valid feelings and the right to those feelings, then some doors open. The young person is much more likely to be willing to explore solutions to the problems causing the pain.

Too often the adolescent does not find that empathy from parents. Too often a parent, with the best of motives, points out early in the conversation what correct assumptions the adolescent is making. Watch such a conversation take place and you can read the adolescent's reactions to the parent on the young face: "I am not being heard, they don't understand me, they think my feelings are ridiculous."

When you believe someone does not appreciate your feelings, do you continue to share with them? Of course not. A die is cast and the parent's influence drops considerably.

When your adolescent does risk sharing with you, keep foremost in your mind the idea that this young person has a right to these feelings — even if you do not agree with them. Your quick reaction may be that this is ridiculous, immature and outlandish thinking. BUT — it is real and valid to the young person thinking and feeling it.

To further ensure understanding during these times of sharing, ask questions with the intent to understand rather than to prove wrong. Try to remember how it felt when you were once rejected, confused, overwhelmed, depressed.

You can set the stage for more sharing by expressing your empathy. Say it. Tell your teenager, "I can understand how you would be upset," "I can remember feeling rejected and when I suffered and it might be like that for you now." "I realize this is very painful for you."

Sometimes parents believe that just listening and trying to understand is really not doing very much to help. But it is. It is opening important doors — both to future sharing and to possible problem solving. After receiving support through a parent's empathy, a young person may be ready to talk about resolving some of the issues of the moment. This kind of dialogue opens the channels for problem solving if the teen is ready for it at that point.

Those families with adolescent siblings have special challenges and rewards. Once again, it is important to remember that adolescents facing similar problems may choose different solutions. That is part of the wonderful process of becoming an individual. Parents should welcome the differences.

By doing so, they help encourage the teenager going through a difficult time to share problems even though his or her siblings are not experiencing the same tough times. The teen who sees himself or herself as "too different" from brothers or sisters may be reluctant to express feelings and yet need to express them even more than others in the family.

Parents with more than one teen in the family need to avoid comparing one teen's "questionable" views with another's "reasonable" ideas. Parents need an extra measure of patience — especially when they have already been through this dialogue with an older son or daughter.

It is always important for parents to respect a teen's confidentiality. Feelings shared with a parent by a teen should be treated as private business.

Teenagers want to be heard by their parents and they want to be heard as respected individuals.

Chapter 8

Self-Esteem vs. Happiness

All parents want their children to feel good about themselves, to possess self-esteem. Experts tell us that self-esteem is the key ingredient in psychological well-being.

How can we help our children build that all-important sense of self-worth?

Many parents themselves have grown to adulthood with the idea that self-esteem is based upon things they do or believe or how one is viewed by their peers. One's self-esteem, this notion goes, depends upon one's achievements, productivity, wealth, religious commitment, kindness, approval from authority or significant others, and on and on and on.

Conditions. That's what those are. This kind of self-esteem, then, is conditional — always dependent upon something we have to do, some mark we have to make. The killer aspect of this line of thought is that lasting self-worth never arrives. It is not enough to meet the mark once — no, to maintain a sense of self-worth, we have to meet it again and again and again.

As parents, we foster this view of self-esteem when we connect achievement or productivity or approval or high morals with self-worth. And we also set our kids up to lose what self-esteem they have. It's a double whammy.

51

When we tie our child's sense of self-esteem to a particular accomplishment and he or she fails to meet the goal, not only is the loss of accomplishment felt — so is the loss of self-worth. He or she is unhappy and down on himself or herself. The unhappiness of the situation is multiplied by the feelings of failure and, "I'm just no good."

There must be another way to promote our children's self-esteem. There is.

It is the unconditional variety. Our children have worth simply because they are who they are. Each is one-of-a-kind, a unique package. That fact alone gives each of them worth.

The acts of achievement, competence, success, morality are all part of who they are. These acts make the child happy — very happy — but they do not measure his or her worth. *The worth is already there.*

The flip side of this approach is that poor performance does not subtract worth. The child — or adult — who fails at an attempted task is not less worthwhile. Less happy, probably, but definitely not less worthwhile.

We are, all of us, human; all of us are fallible. Even with the best of intentions and efforts we are not always going to perform as we'd like.

This separation of self-worth from conditions for happiness is especially important for the adolescent. Adolescence is, after all, a period in life known for its confusion, conflicts, errors in judgment, erratic performances, emotional exaggerations. Tying self-worth to performance adds a pressure especially dangerous to the emotionally vulnerable adolescent.

The situation can be aggravated when the parent's feelings about their own self-worth are tied into their children's performances. The teenager has to do well because Mom and Dad need him to do well for their sense of self-esteem.

Hold up there a minute — that's a pretty heavy load for a kid to carry. Teenager shoulders are not wide enough to support the full weight of an entire family's self-esteem. Under that burden a young person may act out or burn out — perhaps consider suicide.

The parental mistake is not in the valuing of performance and excellence. Not at all. Parents should reinforce and acknowledge their children's competence and achievement, applaud them as good students, musicians, athletes, whatever. The disservice is to attach greater love or acceptance to those achievements.

The parent who connects love to achievement is sending a clear and scary message: "I love you much more when you are doing well."

That parent is inviting adolescent rebellion. That parent is also depriving his or her child of the greatest gift possible — the gift of unconditional acceptance.

The message of unconditional acceptance is this: "I may not agree with or appreciate everything you do, but I always love and value you, no matter what your performances and achievements are.

The adolescent who receives the gift of unconditional acceptance from parents is apt to give the same gift to himself or herself: "My parents accept me for who I am — I can accept me, too."

The opposite view, the conditional view of self-worth is a dangerous spiral that never ends. When a parent's love is conditional, then the teenager's self-acceptance may be conditional, too. And the process of meeting the needs of conditional self-worth is an addiction, a monster that needs constant feeding. The feeling of contentment never lasts because new accomplishment is required to keep self-worth alive.

Because performance will not always peak, self-loathing always waits around the corner. Right beside it is depression: "I did not do well — I am worth nothing — life is worth nothing."

Finally, the teenager who conditions his or her self-worth upon performance is less apt to enjoy strong and happy relationships with other people. Emotional neediness is great for this person because self-worth is always on the line. This kind of neediness fosters possessiveness, dependency, and more pressure than most relationships can withstand.

Chapter 9

Hanging Out

What do you and your teenager do together? What kind of time do the two of you spend?

Take a short trip back in time. Remember when you were an adolescent. Try conjuring up a memory of a pleasant time spent with one of your parents. Details may be a bit fuzzy. It doesn't matter. What does matter is the pleasant recollection of just being together.

Now — back to the present. It is, for any of us, a very purposeful present. We don't want to "waste" time — any time at all.

Many of us use even the time we spend with our children in pursuit of some higher goal, something that will help us grow or develop or achieve. After all, we don't want to waste time.

In the pursuit, we often neglect hanging-out time. Time spent hanging out with the young people in your life is not time wasted. It may not follow the standard definitions associated with "getting things done," but it is a fine way to grow closer and build a relationship that is not an easy one to create.

What is hanging out? Hanging out is nothing more or less than being together with no particular purpose. Oh, usually an activity is involved — fishing, frisbee, bread baking, shopping, garage-sale shopping, biking, eating out, a movie — anything you are both willing to do. The activity, however, is not the goal. Being together is the goal.

The garden doesn't have to get dug or the bread baked or the fish caught. If that happens, that's a bonus. But when the activity becomes a goal, then the focus becomes "getting it done" and the relaxed easy togetherness is lost.

Getting away from good old goal-orientation is tough for a lot of parents: "What are we supposed to do? How do you just 'be'? Do we really have time for this?"

It takes practice but the payoffs are worth it. This kind of time together can breed a bond of mutual appreciation. It is not a time for parents to preach life's lessons or share accumulated wisdom. It is a time for just being.

We cannot make closeness happen, but the kind of closeness we all want with our young people can grow out of something as simple as being together.

Parents with several adolescents have the special task of spending time with each child. Hanging-out time must be individual — even if that means excluding other family members from time to time. Each will get his or her turn and sometimes the entire family will do things together. But there needs to be some time for one parent and one adolescent to just be together.

When you give one-on-one time to each child, you are reinforcing the uniqueness of each. When you don't, you are showing that adolescent similarities outweigh their individual differences. Adolescents do share similarities, but our job is to strengthen the unique relationship we have with each of our children.

Occasionally, an adolescent child will insist that a brother or sister come along on the outing. The teenager may be uncomfortable leaving a sibling behind. Or he or she may simply find the situation of being alone with a parent uncomfortable — especially if it is a rare occurrence. Reassure the uneasy teenager by pointing out that individual time is healthy for each child and for each child's relationship with you.

Many adolescents will resist the suggestion of hanging out with a parent, especially if this kind of togetherness is not an established tradition from earlier years. They resist simply because they are adolescents. The idea sounds boring — it sounds embarrassing. What if someone should see you together?

While parents should be sensitive to their adolescent's feelings, it is all right sometimes to insist. You can lessen the resistance if you give the adolescent some control over where you're going and exactly what form this hanging-out stuff is going to take. Mom wants to take daughter to lunch and shopping at a new shopping center. Daughter says it is a stupid center and Mom negotiates the details of destination.

Giving the teenager some control over the activity tells him or her that what you value is the time together — not the activity itself.

Even if your adolescent is agreeable to the idea, do not expect barrels of enthusiasm. In fact, it is best to expect none, especially in the time right before you're ready to leave. The lack of excitement is not a rejection of you or of the time spent with you. It is an indication of the child's own unsureness about what's coming and how to act. Nothing for you to worry about.

Nor should you expect a mountain of gratitude after the time together is over. It is very likely no word of appreciation will be immediately forthcoming. What is likely, however, is that the experience will be appreciated in retrospect. Ten years from now it will be part of that fond memory file and perhaps one of the building blocks in your solid parent-child relationship.

Teenagers often compare their experiences. Sister Susie may feel that Brother Bobby is having a lot more fun and getting to do a lot more stuff with you than she is.

Listen to what she has to say. You emphasize to the teenager who feels shortchanged that each relationship is unique and impossible to compare. But you listen, too. Explore with the adolescent ways to make this unhappy teen happier: "How can we make this a better experience for you?"

Allow yourself to listen to your child's wisdom. Young people often know what might be helpful. It is our job to ask the questions and listen to the answers.

The benefits of genuine parent-teenager hanging-out time are several. Within families, it reduces sibling competition for parent attention because each child receives a special time and participates in a special relationship. Teens feel a greater sense of their own uniqueness — and parents recognize the individuality of each of their children.

The parent who hangs out with his or her kid will be more apt to find the kid sharing thoughts and feelings. And that same parent will probably have more influence when it comes time to share parental feelings.

The results: a greater closeness between parent and adolescent and a greater tendency toward self-acceptance by the individual adolescent. Both are goals worth working for.

Chapter 10

Special Relationships

Adolescence is not a giant leap in development. It is more of a job — a series of smaller steps, some distinct, some melting into each other.

The parents' best friend along the way is knowledge. If you know what to expect from each step your adolescent takes, you are better armed to respond. And your response is much more likely to be a sound, reasonable one.

Mother-Daughter Relationships

For a mother, the mother-daughter relation is a time of self-examination of thoughts, feelings, and values. It is an awareness of a legacy that is to be passed to the next generation of women. It can often be a time of reciprocal growth. Not only is the teen defining herself, but the mother is awakened to her own sense of being as a female. The daughter is often viewed as an extension of her mother.

Nonetheless, it is important for a mother to recognize just as there may be similarities, there must also be differences. A mother and daughter are unique individuals. There may be similarities in strength and/or imperfections. How they are recognized and dealt with, how they are reconciled is the ultimate responsibility of the individual. A mother may influence and shape but she is not creator. How a mother deals with troublesome qualities can impact on a daughter's self-concept. It is best to be constructive rather than critical or demeaning. It is best to not make love conditional on your daughter's being a certain kind of person. It is indeed possible to accept the individual as you state your own position and disagree with a daughter's position.

Allowing a teen daughter to be her own person is allowing her to exercise her skills in making decisions and choices. This prepares her for separating out from her mother and becoming an independent adult. Frequent questions from a daughter about what you think may be considerate and flattering but they may very well be signs of dependence on your decision-making ability and choices. On the other hand, a rebellious teen daughter who goes out of her way to do the opposite of what you would choose should gently be reminded that she too is being predictably dependent unless she is stopping to think what she herself truly wants rather than reacting. While some daughters may adopt very different values than those of their mothers; more often than not, it is observed that teens return to values of their parents' as adults.

One of the most important opportunities a mother has with her daughter for open communication is during puberty and opposite-sex relationships. The transaction into womanhood with the onset of menses may very well be affected by the education and attitudes exchanged between mother and daughter. Attitudes about males are shaped not only by discussion but by modeling a loving and respectful relation with a spouse or in the case of a single mother, a boyfriend with whom she has a relation. A daughter needs to recognize she owns part of the responsibility in making a relationship work and a responsibility for her own well-being if she is sexually active.

Don't hesitate to state your own beliefs and values but recognize that you will not always be able to control those of your daughter. You have every right to speak up about who you are and why, but it will not guarantee a disciple. Clothes and friends will be claimed as your daughter's own domain and may place you at odds if you place the emphasis on or make that the priority control in your relationship. Mothering has to move beyond control during the teen years if it is to be a quality relation with a limited amount of time for growth before your daughter is out on her own.

Father-Son Relationships

The relationship between father and son during adolescence is two-edged. There are at this developmental time, many opportunities to connect, to share ideas, moments and experiences. At the same time, because the adolescent is forging his own identity and typically focused on peer relationships he can be, at times, unresponsive or oblivious to his relationship with his father. In addition, if Dad has significant expectations of how a son should be at this age and these expectations are not met, this can lead to hurt and anger for both father and son. For example, if Dad needs his son to be an Eagle Scout or a football player and these expectations do not appeal to his son, it can precipitate guilt and anger for the son and feelings of rejection for Dad.

It is not uncommon for a father to expect a son to reflect similar behavior and values of dear old Dad. Respecting a son's uniqueness sets the stage for acceptance of difference. Paradoxically, if a father needs a son to be a certain way, often this need can produce a reaction on the son's part. The son may feel that Dad's acceptance is conditioned or dependent on his being the person his father expects him to be. So it is important to not be too rigid in setting expectations for your son during this time. Accepting his interests and involvements even if they are uniquely different than your interests when you were an adolescent or your interests at the present will help forge this important bond between father and son.

It is also common for a father to be particularly sensitive and/or demanding regarding imperfections that he sees in himself that he wants to see avoided by his son. While this desire on a father's part is understandable, a father should recognize that imperfections and assets are connected to the biological and emotional thread running between both the parents and his child. It is therefore important to accept this as part of the genetic blueprint. Some imperfection similar to Dad's imperfections will occur. Understanding this biological and environmental reality helps a Dad find better acceptance even it it's painful. Viewing them as traits which are part of a package rather than imperfections may also be helpful.

Further complicating father-son relationships during adolescence is a sense of competition that often emerges at this time. This competition is often normal and is not to be taken too seriously by Dad. In fact, it is generally a compliment that a son strive to outdo his father. It is okay to enjoy the competition while constantly seeing that being competitive can be a form of positively connecting. The key is to experience the closeness of being together **while** competing.

Adolescents at times need prodding to spend time with Dad.

Teenage sons are often busy with friends, activities, sports, and jobs. Further, the presence of a father may be a painful embarrassment when a son is with his peers. However, a father should not be put off by a rejection to spend time together: catch small moments such as washing the car together or bigger moments such as going to a baseball game or fishing. These are all important moments in creating a relationship. Collaborating together on things to do, no matter how basic or small, helps encourage togetherness. Additionally, sometimes allowing a son to include a friend in an experience together can also make the activity more fun while not necessarily detracting from its meaningfulness.

Finally, remember fathers influence their relationship with their son by the values and beliefs they communicate by their behavior. When a father takes time to be with a son or his family, he communicates that he feels these people are worth his time — a priority.

Mother-Son Relationships

The relationship between a mother and son during adolescence is often complicated by the many roles a mother plays both in the family and in her son's life. A son generally expects Mom to continue to provide the basics, i.e. meals, laundry, or transportation while at times rejecting her historic role as disciplinarian and confidante.

For many sons adolescence is characterized by feelings of embarrassment when discussing "sensitive or private" issues with a mother. Further, teen males often have difficulty relating to Mom as disciplinarian because of a common perception that Mom doesn't really have the "final say" as the power in the family.

These changes in roles from childhood to adolescence can lead to Mom's feeling used and resentful since she may believe she is no longer playing the significant role in her son's life she once did. Further, as her son begins to normally separate from family and focus on peers, especially female peers, Mom can feel left out or disregarded. She can experience, for example, her son being more thoughtful to peers than to her. A case in point might be a son buying roses on Valentine's Day for his girlfriend but leaving Mom out.

It is important that a mother not withdraw from the relationship with her teenage son because of these developmental changes. Try not to take these changes personally. There are still opportunities for you to connect with your son. You are still in a position for providing guidance and discipline if you approach this task with a low-keyed firmness. Male adolescents often have particular difficulty especially in front of peers accepting loud-confrontive discipline from a mother. It is vital for Mom to remember that her son still likely feels a deep closeness to her that he doesn't dare demonstrate in a loud noticeable way. Most adolescent boys do not have the maturity to publicly hang out with their Mom. A Mom can often find special moments and times of closeness with her son but these special times best occur in private.

Given her historic closeness to her son as a primary caregiver, a mother has a special opportunity for helping a son develop positive values toward women. Since adolescence includes a sizeable interest in females, a mother can help combat "typical" male values that are often reinforced by male society such as female conquest as a key to masculinity. Instead, she can gently help a son see the positive value of having a relationship based on respect, kindness, and sensitivity. A mother has a unique expertise as a female to provide insight and perspective for a son in the area of male-female relationships. Helping a son see that closeness and sensitivity feel better and ultimately pay greater dividends than sexual exploitation is a unique opportunity for a Mom.

A mother who heads a single parent family or a mother in a nuclear family who carries the primary responsibility for childrearing has a unique set of challenges with her son. Admittedly, in households lacking an adult male there will be more sharing of household responsibilities, but it is not uncommon in these families for sons to assume, at times, a helpmate-protector role in relation to their mothers. For a teenage male who normally is working through separation issues during adolescence, this male adult role may very well lead to feelings of resentment and guilt. These feelings can erode the normal connections between mother and son. It is important that a mother recognize the fine line between expecting help from a capable teenage son and depending on him as a male in the absence of a spouse. A teenage son still has dependence needs of his own and wants a parent not a partner.

Father-Daughter Relationships

Nowhere is the importance of development knowledge more clear than in the father-daughter relationship; one of the most special bonds that exists between humans.

During the years of early childhood, daughter and father often discover this special closeness. It is a closeness that includes sharing, mutual admiration, physical expressions of parent-child caring. The little girl grows into middle and late childhood and the special bond

63

runs into competition from friends, teachers, other special adults. Though its expression may change during this time, typically the closeness remains.

In families with several children, this can pose some problems. Built into any sibling situation is competition. It is a feeling amplified in adolescence: teenage brothers and sisters feel they are competing for Dad's love and attention.

Once again, fathers must remember. Each child is unique. Each relationship must also be unique, loaded with its own brand of special interaction.

As the little girl becomes a teenage girl, she enters that time of change we've discussed throughout these pages. Many of the changes are physical and hormonal; puberty is setting in.

It is common during this time — especially in the early stages of adolescence — for a young woman to have erotic feelings about her father or to worry that her father might be sexually interested when hugging her. These are feelings often communicated in very subtle ways.

If Dad picks up these subtle erotic messages, he is apt to panic. He may feel guilty, believing that somehow he has invited these feelings. He has commonly already been struggling within himself to find a way to approach a child in a young woman's body — a child who is very sensitive to changes in her own body being noticed. Sometimes it is easier to not reach out rather than feel awkward or to embarrass. Sadly, he may consequently withdraw from his former closeness with his daughter.

Neither panic nor withdrawal are necessary. First, Dad needs to recognize that one of his adolescent daughter's developmental steps is a new and different fascination with her father. It is normal. Unless it is acted upon, it is absolutely no threat.

The real threat is a father withdrawing from his daughter at a time when she needs him more than ever. Once a father realizes this new sexuality in his little girl is part of the growing-up process, then he is free to find comfortable ways to maintain his closeness with her. He needs to work at continuing a relationship of trust, friendship, protection, and support. That is something she needs from him.

Also, the adolescent girl needs to know that her special relationship with her father can continue; the erotic feelings or concern are not a barrier. Both male and female adolescents need to know that a male-female relationship can be special and trusting without being sexual.

To keep a supportive, trusting relationship going will take some talking and sharing. Father and daughter will have to spend some time talking about their feelings and how they want their relationship to comfortably evolve. It is a time for gentle communication and reassurance. Dad can help his daughter better understand herself and recognize her feelings are normal. He can reassure her that his support and protection and friendship are constants in her life.

It would be helpful for Dad to also spend some time sharing with Mom, too. These are issues the two of them need to discuss. Mom may spot the signals her daughter is sending out or misperceive her husband's feelings about his daughter. It would be easy for her to become jealous — especially if the husband-wife relationship is at all fragile. It is important that Mom recognize the situation as a developmental step and that she supports Dad's handling of matters.

This is admittedly an awkward time for both parent and child. Withdrawal from the whole relationship is a big temptation for the best of fathers. To overcome that temptation, Dad might try some of these basic guidelines.

Physical closeness with your daughter is still okay, as long as it is consistent with your past relationship and as long as the hugs and kisses are clearly paternal.

Be sensitive to signals your daughter sends you. Try asking her how she feels about physical closeness at this time. Share your own sensitivities about the issue.

Often, a teenager will let you know that certain kinds of physical closeness are uncomfortable, even expressions that were perfectly okay just last week may now make her stiffen. When you feel your child shrink from a hug, check it out. Be alert to the child's feelings. If your teenager is uncomfortable with the kiss on the cheek or the hug at the door, do not take it personally. This is not a rejection of you or your affection. It very likely is a reflection of how that teenager is struggling with her own uncomfortable feelings.

The issue is a sensitive one. In no way, however, does it need to destroy the father-daughter bond important to both parent and child.

Conclusion

It is our hope that you have enjoyed this sharing about adolescence. Now, being more understanding of this developmental era do you feel it will go better? It has always been an intent of ours to be helpful to both parents and teenagers. While we emphasize parents owning a sympathetic approach to adolescent development, we believe that reasonable expectations on the part of parents protect them from feeling the upset and pain often associated with adolescence.

With a better understanding of adolescent development, parents will hopefully carefully "pick their battles," realizing that much of what they experience is developmentally based. We believe adolescents continue to require some structure provided by parents. However, that structure will be best if it is an increasing collaboration between parents and adolescents as adolescence unfolds.

Remember a parent never losses their ultimate parental perogative to say no when they collaborate. Thus, a collaboration helps take some of the resistance out of an adolescent's possible reaction while allowing the adolescent to feel more included in the process of decision making. Further, this gives the adolescent the opportunity to learn to make judgments and to profit from their mistakes while still having a parent on board to help guide them through this process.

Finally, it is our hope that with some perspective parents can enjoy watching their teenager blossom. As with everything in life, adolescence is time limited. The bloom only lasts for a period of time and then it is gone forever. This realization will both help us cope as parents and also help us try to do our best during a limited time period and era in our children's and our own lives.

Suggested Readings

The following books may be helpful in giving you additional help in the topical areas listed. These readings will give you more ideas for applications in your life and with your children. Further they will encourage ideas covered in this book.

GENERAL PARENTING

Bruggen, P., & O'Brian, C. (1986). **Surviving Adolescence: A Handbook For Adolescents & Their Parents.** London: Faber & Faber.

*Csikszentmihalyi, M., & Larson, R. (1984). **Being Adolescent: Conflict and Growth in the Teenage Years.** New York: Basic Books.

Davitz, L., & Davitz, J. (1983). **How to Live (Almost) Happily with a Teenager.** New York: NAL.

*Elkind, D. (1984). **All Grown Up and No Place to Go: Teenagers in Crisis.** Reading, MA: Addison-Wesley.

*Elkind, David. (1978). **A Sympathetic Understanding of the Child: Birth to Sixteen.** 2nd ed. Boston: Allyn and Bacon.

*Fine, L.L. (1977). **After All We've Done For Them.** Englewood Cliffs, NJ: Prentice-Hall.

*Gardner, J.E. (1982). **The Turbulent Teens.** Los Angeles: Sorrento.

Gordon, S. (1981). **The Teenage Survival Book: The Complete, Revised, Updated Edition of You.** New York: Times Books.

Herbert, M. (1987). **Living with Teenagers.** New York: Basil Blackwell.

Minton, L. (1972). **Growing Into Adolescence.** New York: Parents' Magazine.

Peterson, A.C. (1987). "Those Gangly Years." **Psychology Today.** September: 28-34

*Showalter, J.E., & Anyan, W.R., Jr. (1979). **The Family Handbook of Adolescence.** New York: Knopf.

*Simon, N. (1982). **"Don't Worry, You're Normal" A Teenager's Guide to Self-Health.** New York: Crowell.

Winn, M. (1983). **Children Without Childhood.** New York: Pantheon.

*cited in chapter What Is Normal.

COPING SKILLS

Barrish, H.H., & Barrish I.J. (1989). **Managing and Understanding Parental Anger.** Kansas City, MO: Westport Publishers.

Burns, D.D. (1981). **Feeling Good: The New Mood Therapy.** New York: William Morrow & Co.

Ellis, A., & Harper, R.A. (1961). **A New Guide to Rational Living.** Englewood Cliffs, NJ: Prentice-Hall.

Ellis, A. (1988). **How to Stubbornly Refuse to be Ashamed of Anything.** Secaucus, NJ: Lyle Stuart.

Ellis, A. (1977). **Conquering Low Frustration Tolerance** (cassette recording). New York: Institute for Rational Living.

Ellis, A. (1977). **How to Live-With-and-Without-Anger.** New York: Reader's Digest Press.

Ellis, A., & Becker, I. (1982). **A Guide to Personal Happiness.** Hollywood, CA: Wilshire Book Co.

Postscript

Surviving Parents —
Helpful Hints For Adolescents

No one said it was going to be easy.

This business of getting through adolescence is no piece of cake. It can be great; it can be the pits.

Hovering around all your highs and lows and in-betweens are those people you once thought knew so much. Your parents.

Along with all the other changes going on in your life, your relationship with them is probably changing, too. Some days you think they make you crazy. Many days you make yourself crazy.

At the bottom of it all, though, you know that life will be saner and more pleasant if you can get along with these two people tied to you like no others. It's not necessarily going to be easy. It definitely is going to be a shared responsibility. You will do better if you spend some effort. You will do better if you learn some coping skills. Your parents have been given the same skills.

There are some tricks to this thing.

The first and toughest is accepting your parent's right to be who they are and act as they do. Warts and all.

Accepting someone — accepting yourself, for instance — includes accepting imperfection. You are sometimes going to screw up. Parents are sometimes going to screw up. Save grief for yourself and

71

for them by not expecting perfection.

What do you expect from them as parents?

Is your expectation an ideal that no human can achieve? Is it a realistic performance that will include mistakes and a number of things you disagree with?

That's another thing about accepting people.

As I've told your parents throughout this book, acceptance does not mean agreement. You can accept your parents and still disagree with their actions, values, judgments and decisions. And you can tell them you disagree.

You are allowed to share your feelings, even when they are not all "yes-you're-right-exactly-right-and-that's-a-fact" kind of feelings.

The key to sharing your opinions and feelings of disagreement with your parents is learning to use what psychologists call an "assertive manner of sharing." Assertive sharing means letting someone know how you feel about the issue on the table and, at the same time, accepting that other person's right to disagree with you.

In fact, this is something you and your parents might discuss at some unemotional, chatty time. Agree to disagree at times.

To accept them and their right to their values and opinions you must give up the idea that they have to agree with you. You can do this with some word choices you use inside your head.

Do not say to yourself, "I **demand** they see things my way."

Say, instead, "I **want** or **prefer** they see things my way."

Go ahead and give it your best shot — be as persuasive as you know how. But keep in mind that they may not end up agreeing with you. And, if agreement isn't demanded by you, it's going to be a lot easier for you to handle the discussion and it's outcome.

Right now is a good time to talk about the difference between, "I don't like it," and, "I can't stand it."

Your parents are going to do and say many things you don't like. They will do few things you think you can't stand.

"You have to be home by 11:00 p.m."

"You cannot go to Emily's party."

You don't like either of those statements. But you can stand them.

Practice recognizing the difference. When you do, you are working on improving your frustration tolerance (another term coined by psychologists).

When you "can't stand" something, you have low frustration tolerance; your ability to cope with difficult situations is reduced. Work on your frustration tolerance and you will have an easier time coping with your parents — and probably in handling other relationships as well.

This brings us to the matter of overreaction. Making mountains out of mole hills. Creating the Big Deal.

You will cope better if you do not exaggerate or blow out of proportion the importance of a given situation with your parents. If you turn a situation — let's say, your brother's getting a fairer shake than you — into a major catastrophe, you are guaranteeing yourself a big emotional upset. It is easy to do.

Read the books about adolescence and they'll tell you the tendency to exaggerate the significance of things is especially strong during this period of life. It's a natural thing to do. Perhaps knowing the tendency is there will help you be alert for it.

When your parents put their feet down, when they say, "You will absolutely not go over to Ben's for the night," you have some choices to make. Is this the end of the world? Is this a major catastrophe? Or is this too bad, unfortunate, disappointing, a pain, unpleasant, regrettable?

It's called putting things in perspective. It takes practice.

Again — it is your right to share your feelings, to try to persuade your parents to change their minds, to let them know how disappointed you are. But, if they still hold firm, then you can choose to keep your disappointment from turning into major rage.

Remember the "warts" mentioned earlier? All parents have them. They are different for different adults just as they are different for different kids.

One parental flaw as you may come across is the hurtful, critical, insensitive word thrown your way in anger. Parents sometimes do that.

They may tell you that you are not measuring up, you've never measured up, you are a big disappointment, you have let everybody down.

What you have to do then is recognize those hurtful words are signposts of your parent's anger and frustration of the moment. These are not words for you to take to heart.

Even if you are sure they mean those words, it does not make the words true.

You can make a monstrous mess of things, a giant mistake. That does not mean you are a bad person. That means you made a mistake. Period. That's all. You may have to pay some consequences, take some punishment. Still, that does not make **you** bad.

Know that there is a difference between who you are and what you do. Remember that. Practice saying it to yourself. It is true.

And, as it is true about you, so is it true about your parents. There is a difference between them as people and the things they do. You can disagree all you like with their actions and judgments and decisions **without** putting them down as people.

If there are brothers or sisters in your family, you can help each other out. Share your concerns about dealing with your parents with them; allow them to share with you. Together you can often be more influential in getting parents to consider your feelings. They may understand exactly how you feel; they may even be able to offer suggestions about dealing with good old Mom and Dad.

Sometimes, of course, the brothers and sisters may be part of the problem you're having with good old Mom and Dad. It may seem to you that each of you is being treated differently and that you are the one getting the short end of the family stick.

At those times, remember that you are each different, each separate individuals, and that you want your individuality respected. Because you are different, your parents are probably going to make different judgments on issues with each of you.

If they don't always seem fair, if they don't always do a good job at that, give them a little room. Remember they will be imperfect but they are trying their best to do right by all of you. They are almost always acting out of their love and caring — no matter how frustrating the acts seem.

What it all boils down to is this: we all have some control over our emotions. We all have some power to limit how upset we are going to be. Practicing some of the suggestions here should help you gain more of that control over emotional upset. And less emotional upset in your life is going to make coping with everything a lot easier.

You are the big winner in this. Oh, sure, your parents will like it if you are easier to get along with. But you are the one who will be less upset less of the time.

And wouldn't that be great?

About the Authors

Harriet H. Barrish, Ph.D. is a licensed psychologist in private practice in Leawood, Kansas.

Dr. Barrish works extensively with parents, families and women in both educational and clinical settings. She is an Associate Fellow of the Institute for Rational-Emotive Therapy in New York and a member of the National Register of Health Service Providers in Psychology.

She is also a past president of the Kansas Psychological Association.

I.J. Barrish, Ph.D. is a Behavioral and Developmental Child Psychologist who is in private practice in Leawood, Kansas.

Dr. Barrish works extensively with children, adolescents, adults and families in both educational and clinical settings.

Dr. Barrish is also an Associate Fellow and Supervisor of the Institute for Rational-Emotive Therapy in New York.

ORDER DIRECT: 1-913-491-4343

❑ YES, I want _____copies of
Managing and Understanding Parental Anger for $6.95 each.

❑ YES, I want _____copies of
Surviving and Enjoying Your Adolescent for $7.95 each.

Please include shipping and handling of $2.50 Book Rate
OR $3.50 UPS for 1st book; 50¢ each additional book.

❑ Check enclosed for $_____ payable to:

Dr. Barrish
4601 College, Suite 270
Leawood, KS 66211

❑ Charge my credit card: ☐ Visa ☐ Mastercard

Acct. # _____Exp. Date_____

Signature_____

SHIP TO:_____

_____

_____

- -

ORDER DIRECT: 1-913-491-4343

❑ YES, I want _____copies of
Managing and Understanding Parental Anger for $6.95 each.

❑ YES, I want _____copies of
Surviving and Enjoying Your Adolescent for $7.95 each.

Please include shipping and handling of $2.50 Book Rate
OR $3.50 UPS for 1st book; 50¢ each additional book.

❑ Check enclosed for $_____ payable to:

Dr. Barrish
4601 College, Suite 270
Leawood, KS 66211

❑ Charge my credit card: ☐ Visa ☐ Mastercard

Acct. # _____Exp. Date_____

Signature_____

SHIP TO:_____

_____

_____

Dr. Barrish
4601 College
Suite 270
Leawood, KS 66211

Dr. Barrish
4601 College
Suite 270
Leawood, KS 66211

ORDER DIRECT: 1-913-491-4343

❏ YES, I want _____copies of
Managing and Understanding Parental Anger for $6.95 each.

❏ YES, I want _____copies of
Surviving and Enjoying Your Adolescent for $7.95 each.

    Please include shipping and handling of $2.50 Book Rate
    OR $3.50 UPS for 1st book; 50¢ each additional book.

❏ Check enclosed for $_____ payable to:

    Dr. Barrish
    4601 College, Suite 270
    Leawood, KS 66211

❏ Charge my credit card: ❏ Visa   ❏ Mastercard

    Acct. # _____Exp. Date_____

    Signature_____

    SHIP TO:_____

    _____

    _____

- -

ORDER DIRECT: 1-913-491-4343

❏ YES, I want _____copies of
Managing and Understanding Parental Anger for $6.95 each.

❏ YES, I want _____copies of
Surviving and Enjoying Your Adolescent for $7.95 each.

    Please include shipping and handling of $2.50 Book Rate
    OR $3.50 UPS for 1st book; 50¢ each additional book.

❏ Check enclosed for $_____ payable to:

    Dr. Barrish
    4601 College, Suite 270
    Leawood, KS 66211

❏ Charge my credit card: ❏ Visa   ❏ Mastercard

    Acct. # _____Exp. Date_____

    Signature_____

    SHIP TO:_____

    _____

    _____

Dr. Barrish
4601 College
Suite 270
Leawood, KS 66211

Dr. Barrish
4601 College
Suite 270
Leawood, KS 66211